I
NSTANT POT MINI COOKBOOK

DEANA DOUGLAS

CONTENTS

CHAPTER 1: GETTING TO KNOW INSTANT POT **8**

THE INSTANT POT COOKING ADVANTAGES 8

DIFFERENT INSTANT POT COOKING SETTINGS 10

OTHER UNIQUE SETTINGS 12

INSTANT POT: DIFFERENT POPULAR MODELS 13

WHICH SIZE IS RIGHT FOR YOU TWO? 14

COOKING TIME CHARTS FOR DIFFERENT INGREDIENTS 15

INSTANT POT COOKING FOR COUPLE'S 22

CHAPTER 2: WHOLESOME BREAKFAST RECIPES **23**

Sweet Potato Hash Morning 23

Squash Cinnamon Porridge 25

Cherry Apple Risotto 27

Pistachio Quinoa Morning 29

Bacon Egg Muffins 31

Cranberry Oats 32

CHAPTER 3: HEALTHY APPETIZERS & SIDES **34**

Sweet Brussels 34

Paprika Potato Appetizer 36

Eggplant Green Side 38

Asparagus Lemon Side 40

CHAPTER 4: INSTANT SOUPS & STEWS **41**

Kale Beef Stew 41

Pork Cabbage Soup 43

Instant Carrot Soup 45

Chicken Ginger Soup 47

Minestrone Pasta Soup 49

Spiced Black Bean Soup 51

CHAPTER 5: HEALTHY GRAINS & RICE MEALS **53**

Buttery Polenta 53

Ham & Rice Treat 55

Potato Lentil Rice 56

Oregano Polenta 58

Cheesy Asparagus Risotto 60

CHAPTER 6: NUTRITIOUS POULTRY MAINS **62**

Rosemary Garlic Chicken 62

Tangy Potato Chicken 64

Lemongrass Coconut Chicken 66

Cola Chicken Wings 68

Classic BBQ Chicken 70

Turkey Tomato Meal 72

Oregano Pasta Chicken 74

CHAPTER 7: WHOLESOME MEAT MAINS **76**

PINEAPPLE PORK 76

GARLIC PULLED PORK 78

SAUCY PORK MEATBALLS 80

OREGANO LAMB SHANKS 81

HONEY GLAZED PORK ROAST 83

CLASSIC BEEF BOURGUIGNON 85

CHEESY MEAT PASTA 87

CHAPTER 8: INSTANT SEAFOOD RECIPES **89**

WINE BRAISED COD 89

JALAPENO PEPPER SHRIMP 91

WHITE WINE HADDOCK 93

TANGY CRABS 95

MUSSELS TOMATINO 96

SWEET CARAMEL SALMON 97

ROSEMARY SALMON 99

CHAPTER 9: SCRUMPTIOUS SNACKS **101**

ARTICHOKE DIP WITH NACHOS 101

CHEESY ASPARAGUS 103

HONEY CARROTS 104

BEAN JALAPENO DIP 106

CHAPTER 10: DELICIOUS DESSERTS **108**

NUTTY CHOCOLATE FUDGE BALLS 108

MOUTHWATERING RAISIN APPLES 110

CHOCOLATE RAMEKINS 111

WONDER WINE PEARS 113

Chapter 1: Getting to Know Instant Pot

Instant Pot is a good investment and is quite a versatile kitchen appliance. It lets you cook food in batches, freeze the cooked meals, and then heat it up later. It has made the task of cooking food easier than ever. Instant Pot seals most of the nutrients in the food and provides you with a nutritionally rich meal at your dining table every day. Let's have a look at what this revolutionary kitchen appliance has to offer.

The Instant Pot Cooking Advantages

Convenient to Operate

As an Instant Pot is programmable, you can easily control it by using different cooking options. Many Instant Pot models can be controlled via Bluetooth making them one of the most advanced cooking appliances. With "Keep Warm" function, you can keep your food warm for as long as you want and can serve it right away without the need to reheat.

No Mess

With Instant Pot, you have a lesser mess to clean and wash after you are done the cooking because you only used one pot for everything. It's got clean in no time.

Energy Efficient & Safe

Many Instant Pot models in the market claim to save around 70% of your electric consumption as compared to traditional cooking methods. Instant Pot is capable of cooking food fast using high pressure steam and generating a high temperature. It reduces the cooking time significantly and helps in saving more electricity. Also, Instant Pot has been designed in a way that the energy it uses is concentrated only on cooking added ingredients to prevent energy wastage.

Multifunctional Appliance

Instant Pot is multifunctional with multiple programmable functions. It acts like a slow cooker, pressure cooker, sauté pot/pan, steamer, warmer, yogurt maker, and rice cooker. It's just one appliance with multiple usages.

Keeps Nutritional Value Intact

Nutritional value of food decreases the longer we cook their ingredients. Instant Pot cooks your food within a just a few minutes. Pressure cooking using Instant Pot only requires a little amount of fluid/water unlike boiling on a regular pot over a stove; thus, it prevents essential nutrients from washing away in remaining water after cooking. Nutritional value is preserved when there's not much fluid needed to tenderize meat and vegetables. Instant Pot uses all the added liquid so that you can get maximum nutrition from meals.

Kills Micro-Organism

In Instant Pot, added water is heated to a high temperature, and it kills most of the unwanted micro-organisms. It kills harmful bacteria and fungus from grains and vegetables to let you enjoy wholesome meals for your whole family.

Different Instant Pot Cooking Settings

Soup

This button is for making broth and soup. Instant Pot's soup function doesn't reach a heavy boiling point, and you have to shred various meats after cooking. The default cooking setting for this particular function is high pressure for 30 minutes.

Meat/Stew

This function is for making various stews and meat-based meals such as beef, pork, lamb, etc. The default cooking setting for this particular function is high pressure for 35 minutes.

Bean/Chili

With this function, you can cook a variety of beans including white beans, kidneys beans, or black-eyed peas. The default cooking setting for this particular function is high pressure for 30 minutes.

Poultry

Poultry meat is generally lighter and faster to cook than pork and beef that is why there is a separate function in Instant Pot. The default cooking setting for this particular function is high pressure for 15 minutes.

Porridge

This setting is for cooking porridges with different kinds of grains. The default cooking setting for this particular function is high pressure for 20 minutes.

Rice

This is the rice cooker setting of Instant Pot. You can use "Adjust" setting to increase or decrease cooking time.

Multigrain

This setting is for cooking a mixture of different grains, brown rice, wild rice, and beans. The default cooking setting for this particular function is high pressure for 40 minutes.

Steam

This function is for steaming vegetables, fish, and other seafood. With this setting, you cannot put the food directly at the bottom of the pot to avoid burning. Use the provided trivet. The default cooking setting for this particular function is high pressure for 10 minutes.

Slow Cook

With this function, you can slow cook from 30 minutes to 20 hours. You can also select between High and Low temperature setting. You can delay cooking time up to 24 hours.

Yogurt

This function is basically for making different kinds of yogurts. The default cooking setting for this particular function is 8 hours. You can use "Adjust" to increase or decrease time.

Keep Warm/Cancel

This setting cancels any program that has been previously. When you press this setting, it automatically sends the cooker in a standby mode and keeps your food warm.

Cake

This setting is for making a variety of cakes.

Egg

This setting is for making a variety of egg-based recipes.

Manual

With this Instant Pot setting, you can manually set your own pressure and cook time.

Sauté

This setting is used for open lid browning, sautéing or simmering of added ingredients. Common ingredients are oil, onions, garlic, etc.

Other Unique Settings

NPR (Natural Pressure Release)

This setting is for naturally releasing pressure for better taste and perfect tenderizing of ingredients. Leave the vent valve alone until it releases all inside pressure gradually; it usually takes 8-15 minutes to release all build up the pressure. After the release of pressure, the silver button on top of the lid goes down.

QPR (Quick Pressure Release)

This setting is for manually releasing the pressure quickly by twisting the vent valve. Use a towel to cover the vent to collect anything that can come out quickly.

PIP (Pot in Pot)

This means the adding another cooking pot or container inside the main cooking pot area. As a result of pressure cooking, the pot does not get as hot as an oven during the baking process. That's why, you are required to use stainless steel, glass, silicone cups or any other oven proof container to add inside the pot, and then you can start cooking.

Instant Pot: Different Popular Models

Lux

Lux in a popular model offering you with two most common sizes of 3, 5 and 6 Quart. However, this option does not provide you to cook with Low pressure, and you need to cook all the recipes using high pressure setting. Some advanced Lux models are offering Bluetooth connectivity using a mobile app.

Lux model is multifunctional and can be used as a rice cooker and slow cooker. It provides many pre-set temperature setting options. It does not have a yogurt making function.

Duo

This model is available in the market in two standard sizes of 3, 6 and 8 Quart and it's most popular among instant pot users. It offers cooking with both low and high pressure setting. Some advanced Duo Plus models are offering Bluetooth connectivity using a mobile app. Duo Plus provides a new blue LCD screen and displays various cooking icons.

Duo model is multifunctional and can be used as a rice cooker and slow cooker. It provides many pre-set temperature setting options. It has pressure cooking options and lets you make yogurts.

Smart

This model is available in the market with the size 6 quart. This model provides you with enhanced control over your cooking technique by providing many customized setting. You can set delay timer for up to 24 hours. It offers cooking with both low and high pressure setting. It comes with an advanced feature of cooking progress indicator.

Smart model is multifunctional and can be used as a rice cooker and slow cooker. It provides 11 pre-set temperature setting options. It has pressure cooking options and lets you make yogurts.

Which Size is Right for You Two?

Don't get confused with the sizes. Remember that you can only fill Instant Pot to its 2/3rd capacity to leave some space for pressure building.

For couples, 3 quart Instant Pot is sufficient. However, if you want to make meals in large proportions to freeze for later use or to make something when you have friends over or a small get to gather, then it is recommended to purchase a 6 quart size model.

Cooking Time Charts for Different Ingredients

Instant pot lets you cook all types of grains and meats within a matter of minutes.

Cooking Time Chart for Various Rice & Grains

Note: Cooking time is mentioned in minutes.

Ingredient Name	Grain/Water Ratio	Cooking Time
Corn, dried, half	1:3	25 – 30
Couscous	1:2	5 – 8
Congee, thin	1:6 ~ 1:7	15 – 20
Congee, thick	1:4 ~ 1:5	15 – 20
Kamut, whole	1:3	10 – 12
Rice, wild	1:3	25 – 30
Porridge, thin	1:6 ~ 1:7	15 – 20
Rice, Brown	1: 1.25	22 – 28
Rice, Basmati	1: 1.5	4 - 8
Quinoa, quick cooking	1:2	8
Rice, Jasmine	1: 1	4 - 10
Rice, white	1: 1.	5 8
Wheat berries	1:3	25 – 30
Oats, quick cooking	1:1	6
Oats, steel-cut	1:1	10
Spelt berries	1:3	15 – 20
Sorghum	1:3	20 – 25
Barley, pearl	1:4	25 – 30
Barley, pot	1:3 ~ 1:4	25 – 30
Millet	1:1	10 – 12

Note: Cooking time is mentioned in minutes.

Ingredient Name	Using Dry Ingredient	Using Soaked Ingredient
Black-eyed peas	20 – 25	10 – 15
Black beans	20 – 25	10 – 15
Chickpeas (chickpeas, garbanzo bean or kabuli)	35 – 40	20 – 25
Cannellini beans	35 – 40	20 – 25
Lentils, yellow, split (moong dal)	15 – 18	N/A
Lentils, red, split	15 – 18	N/A
Lentils, green, mini (brown)	15 – 20	N/A
Lentils, French green	15 – 20	N/A
Navy beans	25 – 30	20 – 25
Kidney beans, white	35 – 40	20 – 25
Kidney beans, red	25 – 30	20 – 25
Soybeans	25 – 30	20 – 25
Scarlet runner	20 – 25	10 – 15
Lima beans	20 – 25	10 – 15
Gandules (pigeon peas)	20 – 25	15 – 20
Anasazi	20 – 25	10 – 15
Adzuki	20 – 25	10 – 15
Great Northern beans	25 – 30	20 – 25

Peas	15 – 20	10 – 15
Pinto beans	25 – 30	20 – 25

Cooking Time Chart for Various Meats

Note: Cooking time is mentioned in minutes.

Ingredient Name	Using Fresh Ingredient
Pork, ribs	20 – 25
Duck cut up with bones	10 – 12
Ham slice	9 – 12
Duck, whole	25 – 30
Ham picnic shoulder	25 – 30
Beef, meatball	10 -15
Beef, stew meat	15 – 20
Chicken, whole	20 – 25
Chicken, breasts	8 – 10
Beef, shanks	25 – 30
Beef, ribs	25 – 30
Chicken, dark meat	10 – 15
Chicken cut up with bones	10 – 15
Cornish Hen, whole	10 – 15
Pheasant	20 – 25
Quail, whole	8 – 10
Veal, roast	35 – 45

Veal, chops	5 – 8
Turkey, drumsticks (leg)	15 – 20
Beef, pot roast, steak, round, chuck	35 – 40
Beef, pot roast, steak, round, chuck	25 – 30
Beef, oxtail	40 – 50
Beef, dressed	20 – 25
Pork, butt roast	45 – 50
Pork, loin roast	55 – 60
Turkey, breast, whole, with bones	25 – 30
Turkey, breast, boneless	15 – 20
Lamb, stew meat	10 -15
Lamb, leg	35 – 45
Lamb, cubes,	10 -15

Cooking Time Chart for Various Vegetables

Note: Cooking time is mentioned in minutes.

Ingredient Name	Using Fresh Ingredient	Using Frozen Ingredient
Collard	4 – 5	5 – 6
Celery, chunks	2 – 3	3 – 4
Cauliflower flowerets	2 – 3	3 – 4
Cabbage, red, purple or green, wedges	3 – 4	4 – 5
Carrots, whole or chunked	2 – 3	3 – 4
Carrots, sliced or shredded	1 – 2	2 – 3
Broccoli, flowerets	2 – 3	3 – 4
Asparagus, whole or cut	1 – 2	2 – 3
Beans, green/yellow, whole, trim ends	1 – 2	2 – 3
Brussel sprouts, whole	3 – 4	4 – 5
Green beans, whole	2 – 3	3 – 4
Corn, on the cob	3 – 4	4 – 5
Corn, kernels	1 – 2	2 – 3
Eggplant, slices or chunks	2 – 3	3 – 4
Beets, small roots, whole	11 – 13	13 – 15

Pumpkin, small slices or chunks	4 – 5	6 – 7
Potatoes, in cubes	7 – 9	9 – 11
Potatoes, whole, large	12 – 15	15 – 19
Okra	2 – 3	3 – 4
Tomatoes, in quarters	2 – 3	4 – 5
Sweet potato, in cubes	7 – 9	9 – 11
Mixed vegetables	2 – 3	3 – 4
Squash, acorn, slices or chunks	6 – 7	8 – 9
Leeks	2 – 4	3 – 5
Peas, green	1 – 2	2 – 3
Artichoke, hearts	4 – 5	5 – 6
Chopped greens including swiss chard, collards, kale, spinach,turnip greens	3 – 6	4 – 7

Cooking Time Chart for Various Fish & Seafood

Note: Cooking time is mentioned in minutes.

Ingredient Name	Using Frozen Ingredient	Using Fresh Ingredient
Lobster	4 – 6	3 – 4
Mussels	4 – 5	2 – 3
Shrimp or Prawn	2-3	1-2
Fish steak	4 – 6	3 – 4
Fish fillet	3 – 4	2 – 3
Fish, whole (trout, snapper, etc.)	7 – 10	5 – 6
Crab	5 – 6	3 – 4
Seafood soup or stock	7 – 9	6 – 7

Cooking Time Chart for Various Fruits

Note: Cooking time is mentioned in minutes.

Ingredient Name	Using Fresh Ingredient	Using Dried Ingredient
Apricots, whole or halves	2 – 3	3 – 4
Apples, in slices or pieces	2 – 3	3 – 4
Peaches	2 – 3	4 – 5
Pears, whole	3 – 4	4 – 6
Pears, slices or halves	2 – 3	4 – 5
Prunes	2 – 3	4 – 5
Raisins	N/A	4 – 5

Instant Pot Cooking for Couple's

When there is just the two of you that need to make plans for your meals, Instant Pot provides the best convenience than any other cooking method. Working couples, be it married or living-in, both remain busy in their jobs and want to save every precious moment to spend with each other after they come home. Even married couples with a wife working as a homemaker, things are no different, when it comes to spending time with each other after work hours.

Instant Pot is handy kitchen equipment that prepares delicious and nutritious food for both of you without demanding your time. You can just add the ingredients and let it do all the cooking, while you can watch TV, go shopping, or complete some pending tasks, while your food gets ready.

Get ready to explore the world of Instant Pot cooking!

Sweet Potato Hash Morning

Prep Time: 5 min.

Cooking Time: 15 min.

Number of Servings: 2

Ingredients:

- 1 cup bell pepper, chopped
- ¼ cup water
- 1 clove minced garlic
- 1 teaspoon paprika
- ½ teaspoon pepper
- 1 medium potato, diced
- 1 tablespoon oil
- 1 medium sweet potato, diced
- Pinch of cayenne
- ½ teaspoon salt
- 1 teaspoon cumin

Directions:

1. In a bowl, toss all the potatoes and pepper in the spices and oil.
2. Switch on your instant pot after placing it on a clean and dry kitchen platform. Add them to the bottom of the pot and add a half cup of water.
3. Close the pot by closing the top lid. Also, ensure to seal the valve.
4. Press "Manual" cooking function and set cooking time to 10 minutes. It will start cooking after a few minutes. Let the pot mix cook under pressure until the timer reads zero.
5. Turn off and press "Cancel" cooking function. Quick release pressure.
6. Open the pot and cook the mixture on sauté mode to brown the potatoes a little more. Serve warm!

Nutritional Values (Per Serving):

Calories - 256

Fat –12g

Carbohydrates – 21.5g

Fiber – 7g

Protein – 4g

Squash Cinnamon Porridge

Prep Time: 15-20 min.

Cooking Time: 8 min.

Number of Servings: 2

Ingredients:

- ½ cup chicken broth
- 2 tablespoons maple syrup
- 2 tablespoons gelatin
- ½ teaspoon ground cinnamon
- ⅛ teaspoon ground ginger
- ⅛ teaspoon ground cloves
- 1 (1¼-pound) whole squash
- 2 medium apples, cored and chopped roughly
- Pinch of salt

Directions:

1. Switch on the pot after placing it on a clean and dry platform.
2. Open the pot lid and place the squash, apples, broth, and spices in the cooking pot area. Give the ingredients a little stir.
3. Close the pot by closing the top lid. Also, ensure to seal the valve.
4. Press "Manual" cooking function and set cooking time to 8 minutes. It will start cooking after a few minutes. Let the pot mix cook under pressure until the timer reads zero.
5. Press "Cancel" cooking function and press "Natural release (NPR)" setting. It will take 8-10 minutes for natural pressure release.
6. Open the pot. Cool down the mixture and then transfer the squash onto a cutting board.
7. Cut the squash in half lengthwise and discard the seeds.
8. In a blender, add the squash, apple mixture from the pot, maple syrup, gelatin, and salt. Blend on a pulse mode until smooth.
9. Serve warm. Enjoy it with your loved one!

Nutritional Values (Per Serving):

Calories - 312

Fat – 0.8g

Carbohydrates – 44g

Fiber – 9g

Protein – 13.5g

Cherry Apple Risotto

Prep Time: 5-8 min.

Cooking Time: 15 min.

Number of Servings: 2

Ingredients:

- ¾ cup risotto rice
- 1 large apple, peeled, cored, and diced
- 1 ½ cups milk
- ¼ cup brown sugar
- ½ cup apple juice
- ¾ teaspoon cinnamon
- ¼ cup dried cherries
- 1 tablespoon butter

Directions:

1. Switch on the pot after placing it on a clean and dry platform. Press "Saute" cooking function.
2. Open the pot lid; add the butter and rice in the pot; cook for 4 minutes to cook well and turn opaque.
3. Mix in the apples, spices, and brown sugar, stirring well to combine. Pour in the milk and juice and stir.
4. Close the pot by closing the top lid. Also, ensure to seal the valve.
5. Press "Manual" cooking function and set cooking time to 6 minutes. It will start cooking after a few minutes. Let the pot mix cook under pressure until the timer reads zero.
6. Press "Cancel" cooking function and press "Quick release" setting.
7. Open and add the dried cherries and stir well.
8. Transfer the mix into bowls and serve with a splash of milk, sliced almonds and a sprinkle of brown sugar.

Nutritional Values (Per Serving):

Calories - 556

Fat – 7g

Carbohydrates – 18.5g

Fiber – 8g

Protein – 10g

Pistachio Quinoa Morning

Prep Time: 1 hour 8-10 min.

Cooking Time: 1 min.

Number of Servings: 2

Ingredients:

- ¾ cup white quinoa
- ⅛ cup raisins
- ½ cup apple juice
- ½ cup plain yogurt
- ½ cup apples, grated
- ½ tablespoon honey
- ¾ cup water
- 1 small cinnamon stick
- ⅛ cup pistachios, chopped
- 3 tablespoons blueberries

Directions:

1. Rinse the quinoa and strain gently using a fine mesh strainer.
2. Switch on the pot after placing it on a clean and dry platform.
3. Open the pot lid and place the water, quinoa and cinnamon stick in the cooking pot area.
4. Close the pot by closing the top lid. Also, ensure to seal the valve.
5. Press "Manual" cooking function and set cooking time to 1 minutes. It will start cooking after a few minutes. Let the pot mix cook under pressure until the timer reads zero.
6. Press "Cancel" cooking function and press "Natural release (NPR)" setting. It will take 8-10 minutes for natural pressure release.
7. Open the pot. Spoon the quinoa into a bowl and remove the cinnamon stick.
8. Mix in the apple, apple juice, raisins, and honey. Refrigerate for at least 1 hour or overnight. Add the yogurt and stir well.
9. Top with the pistachio and blueberries. Serve warm!

Nutritional Values (Per Serving):

Calories - 418

Fat – 6.5g

Carbohydrates – 44.5g

Fiber – 7g

Protein – 14g

Bacon Egg Muffins

Prep Time: 5 min.

Cooking Time: 8 min.

Number of Servings: 2

Ingredients:

- 2 eggs
- ¼ teaspoon lemon pepper seasoning
- 2 crumbled bacon slices
- 1 medium diced onion
- Shredded cheese as needed

Directions:

1. In two silicon molds, separate the cheese, onion, and bacon.
2. Beat one of the eggs and pour it into one of the molds. Repeat the process with the other egg.
3. Switch on the pot after placing it on a clean and dry platform.
4. Pour 1 ½ cup water into the pot. Arrange the trivet inside it; arrange the molds over the trivet.
5. Close the pot by closing the top lid. Also, ensure to seal the valve.
6. Press "Manual" cooking function and set cooking time to 8 minutes. It will start cooking after a few minutes. Let the pot mix cook under pressure until the timer reads zero.
7. Press "Cancel" cooking function and press "Quick release" setting.
8. Open the pot and serve warm. Enjoy it with your loved one!

Nutritional Values (Per Serving):

Calories - 112

Fat – 8g

Carbohydrates – 1g

Fiber – 0g

Protein – 9g

Cranberry Oats

Prep Time: 5 min.

Cooking Time: 15 min.

Number of Servings: 2

Ingredients:

- ½ cup steel cut oats
- ¼ cup orange juice
- 1 tablespoon butter
- 1 tablespoon orange zest
- 1 cup water
- ¼ cup dried cranberries
- ¼ teaspoon vanilla essence
- ¼ teaspoon cinnamon
- 1 ½ teaspoon maple syrup
- 1 cup whole milk

Directions:

1. Take a safe heat bowl and mix in all of the above ingredients.
2. Switch on the pot after placing it on a clean and dry platform.
3. Pour 1 cup water into the pot. Arrange the trivet inside it; arrange the bowl over the trivet.
4. Close the pot by closing the top lid. Also, ensure to seal the valve.
5. Press "Manual" cooking function and set cooking time to 6 minutes. It will start cooking after a few minutes. Let the pot mix cook under pressure until the timer reads zero.
6. Press "Cancel" cooking function and press "Natural release (NPR)" setting. It will take 8-10 minutes for natural pressure release.
7. Open the pot and mix in the berries; serve warm. Enjoy it with your loved one!

Nutritional Values (Per Serving):

Calories - 261

Fat – 6g

Carbohydrates – 11.5g

Fiber – 4.5g

Protein – 9g

Sweet Brussels

Prep Time: 5 min.

Cooking Time: 4 min.

Number of Servings: 2

Ingredients:

- ½ pound Brussels sprouts, trimmed
- 1 tablespoon butter
- 1 ½ teaspoon maple syrup
- Pinch of salt
- 1 teaspoon orange zest
- Pinch of pepper
- 3 tablespoons orange juice

Directions:

1. Switch on the pot after placing it on a clean and dry platform.
2. Open the pot lid and place the above-mentioned ingredients in the cooking pot area. Give the ingredients a little stir.
3. Close the pot by closing the top lid. Also, ensure to seal the valve.
4. Press "Manual" cooking function and set cooking time to 4 minutes. It will start cooking after a few minutes. Let the pot mix cook under pressure until the timer reads zero.
5. Press "Cancel" cooking function and press "Quick release" setting.
6. Open the pot and serve warm. Enjoy it with your loved one!

Nutritional Values (Per Serving):

Calories - 68

Fat – 4g

Carbohydrates – 6g

Fiber – 1g

Protein – 2.5g

Paprika Potato Appetizer

Prep Time: 8-10 min.

Cooking Time: 20 min.

Number of Servings: 2

Ingredients:

- 1 tablespoon dry mango powder
- 2 tablespoons vegetable oil
- 1 teaspoon paprika
- 3 large sweet potatoes, peeled and make wedges
- ½ teaspoon salt
- 1 cup water
- Cooking oil as needed.

Directions:

1. Switch on the pot after placing it on a clean and dry platform.
2. Pour 1 cup water into the pot. Arrange the trivet inside it; arrange the wedges over the trivet.
3. Close the pot by closing the top lid. Also, ensure to seal the valve.
4. Press "Manual" cooking function and set cooking time to 15 minutes. It will start cooking after a few minutes. Let the pot mix cook under pressure until the timer reads zero.
5. Press "Cancel" cooking function and press "Quick release" setting.
6. Open the lid and remove the water. Set aside the potato.
7. Press "Saute" cooking function.
8. Add the oil and potatoes in the pot; cook for 2 minutes to cook well and turn brown.
9. Combine the mango powder, salt, and paprika in a bowl and mix well. Coat the wedges with this mixture and serve warm!

Nutritional Values (Per Serving):

Calories - 164

Fat – 6.5g

Carbohydrates – 25.5g

Fiber – 3g

Protein – 1.5g

Eggplant Green Side

Prep Time: 5 min.

Cooking Time: 5 min.

Number of Servings: 2

Ingredients:

- 2 teaspoons minced garlic
- 1 tablespoon fish sauce
- ½ teaspoon olive oil
- 2 tablespoons soy sauce
- 1 tablespoon oyster sauce
- 1 cup chopped green beans
- 1 cup chopped eggplant
- ½ cup water

Directions:

1. Switch on the pot after placing it on a clean and dry platform. Press "Saute" cooking function.
2. Open the pot lid; add the oil and garlic in the pot; cook for 2 minutes to cook well and turn aromatic.
3. Add the green beans and eggplant to the pot, Mix in the soy sauce, oyster sauce, and fish sauce.
4. Add some water over the vegetables then stir well. Close the pot by closing the top lid. Also, ensure to seal the valve.
5. Press "Manual" cooking function and set cooking time to 3 minutes. It will start cooking after a few minutes. Let the pot mix cook under pressure until the timer reads zero.
6. Press "Cancel" cooking function and press "Quick release" setting.
7. Open the pot and serve warm. Enjoy it with your loved one!

Nutritional Values (Per Serving):

Calories - 46

Fat – 0.5g

Carbohydrates – 9g

Fiber – 3.5g

Protein – 3g

Asparagus Lemon Side

Prep Time: 5 min.

Cooking Time: 2 min.

Number of Servings: 2

Ingredients:

- 2 tablespoons lemon juice
- ¼ pound Asparagus
- 1 cup water
- 1 teaspoon olive oil

Directions:

1. Trim the asparagus and remove the woody parts.
2. Add some lemon juice and olive oil over the asparagus then toss to combine.
3. Switch on the pot after placing it on a clean and dry platform.
4. Pour the water into the pot. Arrange the trivet inside it; arrange the asparagus over the trivet.
5. Close the pot by closing the top lid. Also, ensure to seal the valve.
6. Press "Manual" cooking function and set cooking time to 2 minutes. It will start cooking after a few minutes. Let the pot mix cook under pressure until the timer reads zero.
7. Press "Cancel" cooking function and press "Natural release (NPR)" setting. It will take 8-10 minutes for natural pressure release.
8. Open the pot and serve warm. Enjoy it with your loved one!

Nutritional Values (Per Serving):

Calories – 38

Fat – 2.5g

Carbohydrates – 2.8g

Fiber – 1g

Protein – 2g

Kale Beef Stew

Prep Time: 8-10 min.

Cooking Time: 45 min.

Number of Servings: 2

Ingredients:

- 1 small onion, chopped
- 2 carrots, peeled and chopped
- 1 cups kale leaves, trimmed and chopped
- 1 ½ cups beef broth
- 2 medium potatoes, chopped
- 1 celery stalk, chopped
- 1 tablespoon olive oil
- ½ pound beef stew meat, cut into cubes
- 1 tablespoon hot sauce
- ½ teaspoon garlic powder
- Pepper and salt as per taste preference

Directions:

1. Switch on the pot after placing it on a clean and dry platform. Press "Saute" cooking function.
2. Open the pot lid; add the oil and beef in the pot; cook for 4-5 minutes to cook well and turn browned evenly.
3. Mix in the remaining ingredients. Close the pot by closing the top lid. Also, ensure to seal the valve.
4. Press "Meat/Stew" cooking function and set cooking time to 40 minutes. It will start cooking after a few minutes. Let the pot mix cook under pressure until the timer reads zero.
5. Press "Cancel" cooking function and press "Quick release" setting.
6. Open the pot and serve warm. Enjoy it with your loved one!

Nutritional Values (Per Serving):

Calories - 504

Fat – 15.5g

Carbohydrates – 46.5g

Fiber – 8g

Protein – 42.5g

Pork Cabbage Soup

Prep Time: 15 min.

Cooking Time: 30 min.

Number of Servings: 2

Ingredients:

- 1 small onion, chopped
- 1 cup carrot, peeled and shredded
- 2 cups low-sodium chicken broth
- 1 tablespoon soy sauce
- 1 ½ cups cabbage, chopped
- 1 tablespoon olive oil
- ½ pound ground pork
- ½ teaspoon ground ginger
- Fresh pepper as per taste preference

Directions:

1. Switch on the pot after placing it on a clean and dry platform. Press "Saute" cooking function.
2. Open the pot lid; add the oil and meat in the pot; cook for 4-5 minutes to cook well and turn browned evenly.
3. Mix in the remaining ingredients. Close the pot by closing the top lid. Also, ensure to seal the valve.
4. Press "Manual" cooking function and set cooking time to 25 minutes. It will start cooking after a few minutes. Let the pot mix cook under pressure until the timer reads zero.
5. Press "Cancel" cooking function and press "Quick release" setting.
6. Open the pot and serve warm. Enjoy it with your loved one!

Nutritional Values (Per Serving):

Calories - 294

Fat – 11g

Carbohydrates – 14.5g

Fiber – 3.5g

Protein – 34g

Instant Carrot Soup

Prep Time: 10-15 min.

Cooking Time: 22 min.

Number of Servings: 2

Ingredients:

- ½ teaspoon fresh ginger, minced
- 1 garlic clove, minced
- ½ pound carrots, peeled and chopped
- ½ tablespoon Sriracha
- ⅛ teaspoon brown sugar
- 7-ounce canned unsweetened coconut milk
- 1 cup chicken broth
- 1 tablespoon fresh cilantro, chopped
- 1 tablespoon unsalted butter
- 1 small onion, chopped
- Pepper and salt as per taste preference

Directions:

1. Switch on the pot after placing it on a clean and dry platform. Press "Saute" cooking function.
2. Open the pot lid; add the butter and onions in the pot; cook for 2-3 minutes to cook well and soften.
3. Add the ginger and garlic and cook for 1 minute. Add the carrots, salt, and black pepper and cook for another 2 minutes.
4. Mix in the coconut milk, broth, and Sriracha.
5. Close the pot by closing the top lid. Also, ensure to seal the valve.
6. Press "Manual" cooking function and set cooking time to 6 minutes. It will start cooking after a few minutes. Let the pot mix cook under pressure until the timer reads zero.
7. Press "Cancel" cooking function and press "Natural release (NPR)" setting. It will take 8-10 minutes for natural pressure release.
8. Open the pot and mix in the sugar. With an immersion blender, puree the soup.
9. Serve immediately; top with some cilantro.

Nutritional Values (Per Serving):

Calories – 364

Fat – 30.5g

Carbohydrates – 21.5g

Fiber – 5g

Protein – 6g

Chicken Ginger Soup

Prep Time: 5 min.

Cooking Time: 15 min.

Number of Servings: 2

Ingredients:

- 1-teaspoon ginger
- 2 teaspoons minced garlic
- ½ cup chopped cilantro
- 1-teaspoon cinnamon
- 1-teaspoon coriander
- 1-tablespoon olive oil
- 1-tablespoon sugar
- 1 pound. chopped chicken
- ¼ cup chopped onion
- 3 cups low sodium chicken broth
- 1-tablespoon fish sauce
- ¾ teaspoon salt

Directions:

1. Switch on the pot after placing it on a clean and dry platform. Press "Sauté" cooking function.
2. Open the pot lid; add the butter, garlic, and onions in the pot; cook for 2-3 minutes to cook well and soften.
3. Mix in the chopped chicken, ginger, cilantro, sugar, cinnamon, coriander, fish sauce, and salt.
4. Pour chicken broth and stir gently.
5. Close the pot by closing the top lid. Also, ensure to seal the valve.
6. Press "Manual" cooking function and set cooking time to 15 minutes. It will start cooking after a few minutes. Let the pot mix cook under pressure until the timer reads zero.
7. Press "Cancel" cooking function and press "Natural release (NPR)" setting. It will take 8-10 minutes for natural pressure release.
8. Open the pot and serve warm. Enjoy it with your loved one!

Nutritional Values (Per Serving):

Calories - 288

Fat – 14.5g

Carbohydrates – 23g

Fiber – 2.5g

Protein – 16.5g

Minestrone Pasta Soup

Prep Time: 5-8 min.

Cooking Time: 8 min.

Number of Servings: 2

Ingredients:

- 2 cups chicken broth
- ½ cup elbow pasta
- 14 ounces tomatoes, diced
- 1 cup cooked white beans
- 1 carrot, diced
- 1 teaspoon dried basil
- 1 tablespoon olive oil
- 1 teaspoon dried oregano
- 2 garlic cloves, minced
- 1 bay leaf
- 1 onion, diced
- ¼ cup fresh spinach
- Pepper and salt as per taste preference

Directions:

1. Switch on the pot after placing it on a clean and dry platform. Press "Saute" cooking function.
2. Open the pot lid; add the oil, carrot, onion, garlic, and celery in the pot; cook until turn tender and soft.
3. Add the oregano, basil, pepper, and salt. Mix the tomatoes, spinach, bone broth, pasta, and bay leaf.
4. Close the pot by closing the top lid. Also, ensure to seal the valve.
5. Press "Manual" cooking function and set cooking time to 6 minutes. It will start cooking after a few minutes. Let the pot mix cook under pressure until the timer reads zero.
6. Press "Cancel" cooking function and press "Natural release (NPR)" setting. It will take 8-10 minutes for natural pressure release.
7. Open the pot; add the beans and serve warm. Enjoy it with your loved one!

Nutritional Values (Per Serving):

Calories - 394

Fat – 3g

Carbohydrates – 58g

Fiber – 9.5g

Protein – 20.5g

Spiced Black Bean Soup

Prep Time: 10-12 min.

Cooking Time: 35 min.

Number of Servings: 2

Ingredients:

- 1 tablespoon garlic paste
- 1 tablespoon ginger paste
- 1 teaspoon red chili powder
- ½ teaspoon ground turmeric
- ½ teaspoon garam masala
- 2 teaspoons ground coriander
- 1 tablespoon olive oil
- 1 teaspoon cumin seeds
- 1 medium onion, chopped
- Salt as per taste preference
- 1 cup black beans, soaked overnight and drained
- 2 cups water
- 1 teaspoon lemon juice

Directions:

1. Switch on the pot after placing it on a clean and dry platform. Press "Sauté" cooking function.
2. Open the pot lid; add the oil and cumin seeds in the pot; cook for 30 seconds.
3. Add the onion, garlic, spices, and ginger; cook for 3-4 minutes to cook well and soften.
4. Mix in the chickpeas and water. Close the pot by closing the top lid. Also, ensure to seal the valve.
5. Press "Bean/Chili" cooking function and set cooking time to 30 minutes. It will start cooking after a few minutes. Let the pot mix cook under pressure until the timer reads zero.
6. Press "Cancel" cooking function and press "Natural release (NPR)" setting. It will take 8-10 minutes for natural pressure release.
7. Open the pot; mix the lemon juice and serve warm. Enjoy it with your loved one!

Nutritional Values (Per Serving):

Calories - 437

Fat – 9g

Carbohydrates – 68.5g

Fiber – 16.5g

Protein – 22g

Buttery Polenta

Prep Time: 5 min.

Cooking Time: 8 min.

Number of Servings: 2

Ingredients:

- ½ cup polenta
- ½ teaspoon salt
- 2 cup milk
- 3 tablespoons milk
- 3 tablespoons butter

Directions:

1. Switch on the pot after placing it on a clean and dry platform. Press "Sauté" cooking function.
2. Open the pot lid; add the milk and boil it. Mix in the polenta with the salt.
3. Close the pot by closing the top lid. Also, ensure to seal the valve.
4. Press "Manual" cooking function and set cooking time to 8 minutes. It will start cooking after a few minutes. Let the pot mix cook under pressure until the timer reads zero.
5. Press "Cancel" cooking function and press "Quick release" setting.
6. Open the pot; mix 3 tablespoons of milk and butter.
7. Serve warm. Enjoy it with your loved one!

Nutritional Values (Per Serving):

Calories - 147

Fat – 2g

Carbohydrates – 22.5g

Fiber – 2.5g

Protein – 12g

Ham & Rice Treat

Prep Time: 2 min.

Cooking Time: 6 min.

Number of Servings: 2

Ingredients:

- ½ cup ham, diced
- 1 ½ cup brown rice
- 1 tablespoon butter
- 2 tablespoons scallions, sliced
- ½ cup matchstick carrots
- 1 ½ cup water
- 1 tablespoon soy sauce

Directions:

1. Switch on the pot after placing it on a clean and dry platform.
2. Open the pot lid and put the above-mentioned ingredients in the cooking pot area. Give the ingredients a little stir.
3. Close the pot by closing the top lid. Also, ensure to seal the valve.
4. Press "Manual" cooking function and set cooking time to 6 minutes. It will start cooking after a few minutes. Let the pot mix cook under pressure until the timer reads zero.
5. Press "Cancel" cooking function and press "Quick release" setting.
6. Open the pot; fluff the mix and serve warm. Enjoy it with your loved one!

Nutritional Values (Per Serving):

Calories - 116

Fat – 6g

Carbohydrates – 12g

Fiber – 2.5g

Protein – 4g

Potato Lentil Rice

Prep Time: 8-10 min.

Cooking Time: 10 min.

Number of Servings: 2

Ingredients:

- ½ tablespoon ginger paste
- 1 small potato, cut into small pieces
- ½ cup white rice, rinsed
- ½ cup split green lentils, rinsed
- 3 cups water
- 1 tomato, chopped finely
- ¼ teaspoon red chili powder
- ¼ teaspoon ground turmeric
- 1 tablespoon fresh cilantro, chopped
- ½ cup carrots, peeled and diced
- ½ cup fresh green peas, shelled
- 1 tablespoon olive oil
- ½ teaspoon cumin seeds
- ½ of a small onion, chopped
- Salt as per taste preference

Directions:

1. Switch on the pot after placing it on a clean and dry platform. Press "Sauté" cooking function.
2. Open the pot lid; add the oil and cumin seeds and cook for 30 seconds.
3. Add the onions and ginger and cook for about 2 minutes. Add the vegetables and spices and cook for 2 minutes.
4. Mix in other ingredients and stir well. Do not add the cilantro.
5. Close the pot by closing the top lid. Also, ensure to seal the valve.
6. Press "Manual" cooking function and set cooking time to 5 minutes. It will start cooking after a few minutes. Let the pot mix cook under pressure until the timer reads zero.
7. Press "Cancel" cooking function and press "Natural release (NPR)" setting. It will take 8-10 minutes for natural pressure release.

8. Open the pot; top with the cilantro and serve warm. Enjoy it with your loved one!

Nutritional Values (Per Serving):

Calories – 358

Fat – 16g

Carbohydrates – 55.5g

Fiber – 11g

Protein – 20g

Oregano Polenta

Prep Time: 5 min.

Cooking Time: 8-10 min.

Number of Servings: 2

Ingredients:

- 1 bunch green onions
- 2 tablespoons cilantro
- 1 cup broth
- ½ teaspoon oregano
- 1 ½ teaspoon chili powder
- ¼ teaspoon paprika
- ½ teaspoon cumin
- 1 cup boiling water
- ½ cup cornmeal
- 1 teaspoon garlic, minced
- Pinch of cayenne

Directions:

1. Switch on the pot after placing it on a clean and dry platform. Press "Sauté" cooking function.
2. Open the pot lid; add some cooking oil, garlic, and onions in the pot; cook for 2-3 minutes to cook well and soften.
3. Mix in the broth, cilantro, cornmeal, spices and boiling water. Close the pot by closing the top lid. Also, ensure to seal the valve.
4. Press "Manual" cooking function and set cooking time to 5 minutes. It will start cooking after a few minutes. Let the pot mix cook under pressure until the timer reads zero.
5. Press "Cancel" cooking function and press "Natural release (NPR)" setting. It will take 8-10 minutes for natural pressure release.
6. Open the pot and serve warm. Enjoy it with your loved one!

Nutritional Values (Per Serving):

Calories - 98

Fat – 1.5g

Carbohydrates – 6g

Fiber – 3g

Protein – 4g

Cheesy Asparagus Risotto

Prep Time: 5 min.

Cooking Time: 15 min.

Number of Servings: 2

Ingredients:

- 1 small onion, chopped
- 1 tablespoon olive oil
- 1 tablespoon thyme
- ½ cup risotto rice
- 2 garlic cloves, chopped
- ¼ cup parmesan, grated
- 2 tablespoons orange juice
- ½ pound asparagus, diced
- 1 1/3 cup vegetable stock

Directions:

1. Switch on the pot after placing it on a clean and dry platform. Press "Sauté" cooking function.
2. Open the pot lid; add the oil and onions in the pot; cook for 2 minutes to cook well and soften.
3. Mix the rice and the garlic; cook until the garlic becomes fragrant. Mix in the stock and the orange juice.
4. Close the pot by closing the top lid. Also, ensure to seal the valve.
5. Press "Manual" cooking function and set cooking time to 7 minutes. It will start cooking after a few minutes. Let the pot mix cook under pressure until the timer reads zero.
6. Press "Cancel" cooking function and press "Quick release" setting.
7. Open the pot and mix the thyme and asparagus. Do not cover, let it sit for 5-8 more minutes for asparagus to soften.
8. Place in a serving bowl and top with the cheese. Serve warm!

Nutritional Values (Per Serving):

Calories - 436

Fat – 15g

Carbohydrates – 44.5g

Fiber – 4g

Protein – 24g

Rosemary Garlic Chicken

Prep Time: 5-8 min.

Cooking Time: 10 min.

Number of Servings: 2

Ingredients:

- 2 tablespoons minced garlic
- 1-cup low sodium chicken broth
- 1 ½ teaspoons olive oil
- ¾ pound chopped boneless chicken
- ½ cup chopped onion
- ¼ teaspoon thyme
- ½ teaspoon salt
- ½ teaspoon pepper
- 1 bay leaf
- 1 tablespoon chopped rosemary
- 2 tablespoons chopped celery

Directions:

1. Switch on the pot after placing it on a clean and dry platform. Press "Sauté" cooking function.
2. Open the pot lid; add the oil, garlic, and onions in the pot; cook for 2 minutes to cook well and turn lightly golden.
3. Add chicken cubes to the pot. Mix the salt, pepper, bay leaf, chopped rosemary, and thyme.
4. Close the pot by closing the top lid. Also, ensure to seal the valve.
5. Press "Manual" cooking function and set cooking time to 10 minutes. It will start cooking after a few minutes. Let the pot mix cook under pressure until the timer reads zero.
6. Press "Cancel" cooking function and press "Natural release (NPR)" setting. It will take 8-10 minutes for natural pressure release.

7. Open the pot; topped with some celery and serve warm. Enjoy it with your loved one!

Nutritional Values (Per Serving):

Calories - 176

Fat – 8g

Carbohydrates – 7.5g

Fiber – 2g

Protein – 17g

Tangy Potato Chicken

Prep Time: 8-10 min.

Cooking Time: 20 min.

Number of Servings: 2

Ingredients:

- ½ cup low sodium chicken broth
- 1-½ tablespoons Dijon mustard
- 1 tablespoon Italian seasoning
- 2 tablespoons lemon juice
- 1 teaspoon lemon zest
- 1 pound. chopped chicken
- 1 pound potatoes, peeled and make wedges
- ½ teaspoon salt
- ½ teaspoon pepper

Directions:

1. Season the chicken with pepper and salt. Switch on the pot after placing it on a clean and dry platform.
2. Open the pot lid and place the above-mentioned ingredients in the cooking pot area. Give the ingredients a little stir.
3. Close the pot by closing the top lid. Also, ensure to seal the valve.
4. Press "Manual" cooking function and set cooking time to 15 minutes. It will start cooking after a few minutes. Let the pot mix cook under pressure until the timer reads zero.
5. Press "Cancel" cooking function and press "Natural release (NPR)" setting. It will take 8-10 minutes for natural pressure release.
6. Open the pot and serve warm. Enjoy it with your loved one!

Nutritional Values (Per Serving):

Calories - 256

Fat – 3.5g

Carbohydrates – 34.5g

Fiber – 6g

Protein – 18.5g

Lemongrass Coconut Chicken

Prep Time: 5 min.

Cooking Time: 15 min.

Number of Servings: 2

Ingredients:

- 2 teaspoons minced garlic
- 3 teaspoons fish sauce
- ¼ teaspoon pepper
- 1 tablespoon lemon juice
- ¼ cup chopped onion
- 1 lemongrass
- 1-teaspoon ginger
- 4 chicken drumsticks
- ½ teaspoon coconut oil
- ¾ cup coconut milk

Directions:

1. Chop the lemongrass and add in a blender. Add the garlic, ginger, fish sauce, pepper, and lemon juice; combine well.
2. Add the coconut milk. Blend until smooth and incorporated.
3. Switch on the pot after placing it on a clean and dry platform. Press "Sauté" cooking function.
4. Open the pot lid; add the oil and onions in the pot; cook for 2 minutes to cook well and soften.
5. Add the drumsticks to the pot; top with the coconut mixture over the chicken.
6. Close the pot by closing the top lid. Also, ensure to seal the valve.
7. Press "Manual" cooking function and set cooking time to 10 minutes. It will start cooking after a few minutes. Let the pot mix cook under pressure until the timer reads zero.
8. Press "Cancel" cooking function and press "Natural release (NPR)" setting. It will take 8-10 minutes for natural pressure release.
9. Open the pot and serve warm. Enjoy it with your loved one!

Nutritional Values (Per Serving):

Calories - 342

Fat – 28.5g

Carbohydrates – 9.5g

Fiber – 2.5g

Protein – 13g

Cola Chicken Wings

Prep Time: 8-10 min.

Cooking Time: 20 min.

Number of Servings: 2

Ingredients:

- 2 tablespoons chopped onion
- 1-½ tablespoons low sodium soy sauce
- ½ tablespoon rice wine
- ½ tablespoon sesame oil
- ½ teaspoon ginger
- 1 cup your choice of cola
- 1 pound. chicken wings
- 2 teaspoons minced garlic

Directions:

1. Switch on the pot after placing it on a clean and dry platform. Press "Sauté" cooking function.
2. Open the pot lid; add the oil, garlic, and onions in the pot; cook for 2 minutes to cook well and soften.
3. Add the chicken wings and sauté until brown. Mix in the cola, soy sauce, and rice wine then stir well.
4. Close the pot by closing the top lid. Also, ensure to seal the valve.
5. Press "Manual" cooking function and set cooking time to 20 minutes. It will start cooking after a few minutes. Let the pot mix cook under pressure until the timer reads zero.
6. Press "Cancel" cooking function and press "Natural release (NPR)" setting. It will take 8-10 minutes for natural pressure release.
7. Open the pot and serve warm. Enjoy it with your loved one!

Nutritional Values (Per Serving):

Calories - 228

Fat – 8.5g

Carbohydrates – 32g

Fiber – 0.5g

Protein – 5.5g

Classic BBQ Chicken

Prep Time: 5 min.

Cooking Time: 15 min.

Number of Servings: 2

Ingredients:

- 1-cup water
- ½ cup chopped onion
- 2-½ tablespoons raw honey
- 2 pounds. chicken wings
- ½ cup barbecue sauce
- ¼ teaspoon salt
- ½ teaspoon pepper

Directions:

1. In a bowl, mix the barbecue sauce with water, raw honey, salt, and pepper. Switch on the pot after placing it on a clean and dry platform.
2. Open the pot lid and place the chicken and sauce in the cooking pot area. Give the ingredients a little stir.
3. Close the pot by closing the top lid. Also, ensure to seal the valve.
4. Press "Manual" cooking function and set cooking time to 10 minutes. It will start cooking after a few minutes. Let the pot mix cook under pressure until the timer reads zero.
5. Press "Cancel" cooking function and press "Quick release" setting.
6. Open the pot.
7. Preheat a pan over medium heat; add the chicken mix to the pan. Bring to simmer and stir until the barbecue sauce is thickened.
8. Serve warm!

Nutritional Values (Per Serving):

Calories – 334

Fat – 10g

Carbohydrates – 45g

Fiber – 1.5g

Protein – 10.5g

Turkey Tomato Meal

Prep Time: 8-10 min.

Cooking Time: 20 min.

Number of Servings: 2

Ingredients:

- 1 red onion, sliced
- 1 cup chicken stock
- 1 tablespoon butter
- 1 red bell pepper, chopped
- 1 green bell pepper, chopped
- 2 pounds ground turkey breast
- 1 15-ounce can of diced tomatoes
- 2 cloves garlic, chopped

Directions:

1. Switch on the pot after placing it on a clean and dry platform. Press "Sauté" cooking function.
2. Open the pot lid; add the butter and meat in the pot; cook for 5 minutes to cook well and soften.
3. Add the tomatoes with their juices, garlic, onion, peppers, and stock.
4. Close the pot by closing the top lid. Also, ensure to seal the valve.
5. Press "Manual" cooking function and set cooking time to 15 minutes. It will start cooking after a few minutes. Let the pot mix cook under pressure until the timer reads zero.
6. Press "Cancel" cooking function and press "Quick release" setting.
7. Open the pot and serve warm. Enjoy it with your loved one!

Nutritional Values (Per Serving):

Calories - 506

Fat – 19.5g

Carbohydrates – 12g

Fiber – 2.5g

Protein – 62.5g

Oregano Pasta Chicken

Prep Time: 5 min.

Cooking Time: 15 min.

Number of Servings: 2

Ingredients:

- ½ teaspoon olive oil
- ½ cup diced tomatoes
- ½ cup diced red bell pepper
- ½ teaspoon oregano
- 1 bay leaf
- ½ cup chopped onion
- 1 ½ cup diced chicken
- ¼ teaspoon salt
- ½ teaspoon pepper
- 2 tablespoons chopped parsley
- Cooked pasta of your choice

Directions:

1. Switch on the pot after placing it on a clean and dry platform. Press "Sauté" cooking function.
2. Open the pot lid; add the oil and onions in the pot; cook for 2 minutes to cook well and soften.
3. Add the chicken, bell pepper, and diced tomatoes. Mix the salt, pepper, oregano, and bay leaf.
4. Close the pot by closing the top lid. Also, ensure to seal the valve.
5. Press "Manual" cooking function and set cooking time to 10 minutes. It will start cooking after a few minutes. Let the pot mix cook under pressure until the timer reads zero.
6. Press "Cancel" cooking function and press "Natural release (NPR)" setting. It will take 8-10 minutes for natural pressure release.
7. Open the pot; top with some parsley and serve with cooked pasta!

Nutritional Values (Per Serving):

Calories - 102

Fat – 2.5g

Carbohydrates – 4g

Fiber – 1g

Protein – 15.5g

Pineapple Pork

Prep Time: 8-10 min.

Cooking Time: 25 min.

Number of Servings: 2

Ingredients:

- 1 cup unsweetened pineapple juice
- ½ cup pineapple chunks
- ½ teaspoon nutmeg
- ½ teaspoon cinnamon
- 2 cloves
- ¼ cup chopped onion
- ½ teaspoon rosemary
- ½ pounds. pork tenderloin, sliced
- ½ cup tomato puree

Directions:

1. Switch on the pot after placing it on a clean and dry platform.
2. Open the pot lid and place the above-mentioned ingredients in the cooking pot area. Give the ingredients a little stir. Do not add the chunks.
3. Close the pot by closing the top lid. Also, ensure to seal the valve.
4. Press "Manual" cooking function and set cooking time to 25 minutes. It will start cooking after a few minutes. Let the pot mix cook under pressure until the timer reads zero.
5. Press "Cancel" cooking function and press "Quick release" setting.
6. Open the pot; add the chunks and serve warm. Enjoy it with your loved one!

Nutritional Values (Per Serving):

Calories - 292

Fat – 5g

Carbohydrates – 30g

Fiber – 3.5g

Protein – 31.5g

Garlic Pulled Pork

Prep Time: 8-10 min.

Cooking Time: 40 min.

Number of Servings: 2

Ingredients:

- ¼ teaspoon salt
- 1-tablespoon cornstarch
- 3 tablespoons water
- ½ cup beef broth
- ½ cup chopped onion
- 1 pound pork belly, make cubes
- 1 ½ teaspoons black pepper
- 1-teaspoon thyme

Directions:

1. Switch on the pot after placing it on a clean and dry platform.
2. Open the pot lid and place the above-mentioned ingredients in the cooking pot area. Give the ingredients a little stir. Do not add the water and cornstarch.
3. Close the pot by closing the top lid. Also, ensure to seal the valve.
4. Press "Manual" cooking function and set cooking time to 35 minutes. It will start cooking after a few minutes. Let the pot mix cook under pressure until the timer reads zero.
5. Press "Cancel" cooking function and press "Quick release" setting.
6. Open the pot. Combine cornstarch with water then stir into the Instant Pot.
7. Add the liquid over the pork then serve warm!

Nutritional Values (Per Serving):

Calories - 188

Fat – 15g

Carbohydrates – 8g

Fiber – 1.5g

Protein – 4.5g

Saucy Pork Meatballs

Prep Time: 8-10 min.

Cooking Time: 25 min.

Number of Servings: 2

Ingredients:

- 1 tablespoon breadcrumb
- ¼ cup coconut milk
- ¾ teaspoon brown sugar
- ¾ pounds. ground pork
- ¼ cup chopped onion
- 1 organic egg

Directions:

1. Combine the meat with egg and breadcrumbs. Shape the mixture into balls.
2. Switch on the pot after placing it on a clean and dry platform.
3. Open the pot lid and place the balls and milk in the cooking pot area. Add the brown sugar and chopped onion. Give the ingredients a little stir.
4. Close the pot by closing the top lid. Also, ensure to seal the valve.
5. Press "Manual" cooking function and set cooking time to 25 minutes. It will start cooking after a few minutes. Let the pot mix cook under pressure until the timer reads zero.
6. Press "Cancel" cooking function and press "Natural release (NPR)" setting. It will take 8-10 minutes for natural pressure release.
7. Open the pot and serve warm. Enjoy it with your loved one!

Nutritional Values (Per Serving):

Calories - 272

Fat – 21g

Carbohydrates – 6.5g

Fiber – 1.5g

Protein – 13.5g

Oregano Lamb Shanks

Prep Time: 10 min.

Cooking Time: 35 min.

Number of Servings: 2

Ingredients:

- 2 garlic cloves, diced
- 1 large onion, chopped
- 1 tomato, diced
- 1 teaspoon oregano
- 1 cup red wine
- 3 carrots, diced
- 2 tablespoons tomato paste
- 2 pounds lamb shanks
- 4 tablespoons white flour
- 2 tablespoons olive oil
- ½ cup beef stock
- Pepper and salt as per taste preference

Directions:

1. In a bowl, mix the flour, salt, and pepper. Add the shanks and coat well with the flour.
2. Switch on the pot after placing it on a clean and dry platform. Press "Sauté" cooking function.
3. Open the pot lid; add the oil and lamb in the pot; cook for 2 minutes to cook well and browned. Set aside.
4. In the remaining hot oil, sauté the garlic and onion for 4-5 minutes. Mix in the tomato paste, tomato, red wine, and beef stock. Boil the mixture.
5. Add the shanks. Close the pot by closing the top lid. Also, ensure to seal the valve.
6. Press "Manual" cooking function and set cooking time to 25 minutes. It will start cooking after a few minutes. Let the pot mix cook under pressure until the timer reads zero.
7. Press "Cancel" cooking function and press "Natural release (NPR)" setting. It will take 8-10 minutes for natural pressure release.

8. Open the pot and serve warm. Enjoy it with your loved one!

Nutritional Values (Per Serving):

Calories - 611

Fat – 24g

Carbohydrates – 18g

Fiber – 2.5g

Protein – 63.5g

Honey Glazed Pork Roast

Prep Time: 5 min.

Cooking Time: 35 min.

Number of Servings: 2

Ingredients:

- 2 tablespoons raw honey
- 1/2 tablespoon dry basil
- ½ tablespoon cornstarch
- ½ cup water
- ½ tablespoon garlic, minced
- ½ tablespoon olive oil
- 1 pound pork roast
- 2 tablespoons parmesan cheese, grated
- 1 tablespoon soy sauce
- Salt as per taste preference

Directions:

1. Switch on the pot after placing it on a clean and dry platform.
2. Open the pot lid and place the above-mentioned ingredients in the cooking pot area. Give the ingredients a little stir.
3. Close the pot by closing the top lid. Also, ensure to seal the valve.
4. Press "Meat" cooking function and set cooking time to 35 minutes. It will start cooking after a few minutes. Let the pot mix cook under pressure until the timer reads zero.
5. Press "Cancel" cooking function and press "Natural release (NPR)" setting. It will take 8-10 minutes for natural pressure release.
6. Open the pot and serve warm. Enjoy it with your loved one!

Nutritional Values (Per Serving):

Calories - 652

Fat – 29.5g

Carbohydrates – 20g

Fiber – 0.5g

Protein – 68g

Classic Beef Bourguignon

Prep Time: 10 min.

Cooking Time: 40 min.

Number of Servings: 2

Ingredients:

- 1 medium onion, chopped
- 1 tablespoon thyme
- ½ cup beef stock
- ½ cup red wine
- 2 medium carrots, chopped
- 1 tablespoon parsley
- ½ pound beef stew meat
- 2 bacon slices
- 1 garlic clove, minced
- 1 large potato, cubed
- ½ tablespoon honey
- ½ tablespoon olive oil

Directions:

1. Switch on the pot after placing it on a clean and dry platform. Press "Sauté" cooking function.
2. Open the pot lid; add the oil and beef in the pot; cook for 3-4 minutes to cook well and evenly browned. Set aside.
3. Add the bacon and onion, and sauté until onion is translucent. Add beef and the rest of the ingredients.
4. Close the pot by closing the top lid. Also, ensure to seal the valve.
5. Press "Manual" cooking function and set cooking time to 30 minutes. It will start cooking after a few minutes. Let the pot mix cook under pressure until the timer reads zero.
6. Press "Cancel" cooking function and press "Natural release (NPR)" setting. It will take 8-10 minutes for natural pressure release.
7. Open the pot and serve warm. Enjoy it with your loved one!

Nutritional Values (Per Serving):

Calories - 558

Fat – 16.5g

Carbohydrates – 46.5g

Fiber – 7g

Protein – 42g

Cheesy Meat Pasta

Prep Time: 5 min.

Cooking Time: 8-10 min.

Number of Servings: 2

Ingredients:

- 4 ounces mozzarella cheese
- 1 cup pasta sauce
- 1 cup water
- ¼ pound ground beef
- ¼ pound ground pork
- 6 ounces ruffles pasta
- 4 ounces ricotta cheese
- Cooking oil

Directions:

1. Switch on the pot after placing it on a clean and dry platform. Press "Sauté" cooking function.
2. Open the pot lid; add the oil, pork, and beef in the pot; cook for 3-4 minutes to cook well and evenly browned.
3. Mix the water, pasta, and sauce.
4. Close the pot by closing the top lid. Also, ensure to seal the valve.
5. Press "Manual" cooking function and set cooking time to 5 minutes. It will start cooking after a few minutes. Let the pot mix cook under pressure until the timer reads zero.
6. Press "Cancel" cooking function and press "Quick release" setting.
7. Open the pot, mix the cheese and serve warm. Enjoy it with your loved one!

Nutritional Values (Per Serving):

Calories - 588

Fat – 24g

Carbohydrates – 52.5g

Fiber – 4.5g

Protein – 61g

Wine Braised Cod

Prep Time: 5 min.

Cooking Time: 5 min.

Number of Servings: 2

Ingredients:

- 1 cup white wine
- 1 teaspoon oregano
- 1 sprig fresh rosemary
- 2 garlic cloves, smashed
- 1 teaspoon paprika
- 1 pound cod, cut into 4 filets
- 1 bag (10 ounces) frozen peas
- 1 cup fresh parsley

Pepper and salt as per taste preference

Directions:

1. In a bowl, mix the wine, herbs, salt, and spices together.
2. Add the liquid into the Instant Pot and add the peas.
3. Arrange the fish into a steamer basket and lower it to the liquid.
4. Close the pot by closing the top lid. Also, ensure to seal the valve.
5. Press "Manual" cooking function and set cooking time to 5 minutes. It will start cooking after a few minutes. Let the pot mix cook under pressure until the timer reads zero.
6. Press "Cancel" cooking function and press "Quick release" setting.
7. Open the pot and serve warm. Enjoy it with your loved one!

Nutritional Values (Per Serving):

Calories - 234

Fat – 1.5g

Carbohydrates – 13.5g

Fiber – 44g

Protein – 30g

Jalapeno Pepper Shrimp

Prep Time: 8-10 min.

Cooking Time: 5 min.

Number of Servings: 2

Ingredients:

- 1 teaspoon white pepper
- 1 teaspoon cayenne pepper
- 2 cloves garlic, minced
- 1 sweet onion, minced
- 1 can diced tomatoes (15 ounces)
- 1 jalapeno pepper, minced
- 1 pound frozen shrimp, peeled and deveined
- 1 lemon, juiced
- 1 teaspoon black pepper

Directions:

1. Allow the frozen shrimp to rest at room temperature for 15 minutes. Switch on the pot after placing it on a clean and dry platform.
2. Open the pot lid and place the above-mentioned ingredients in the cooking pot area. Give the ingredients a little stir.
3. Close the pot by closing the top lid. Also, ensure to seal the valve.
4. Press "Manual" cooking function and set cooking time to 5 minutes. It will start cooking after a few minutes. Let the pot mix cook under pressure until the timer reads zero.
5. Press "Cancel" cooking function and press "Quick release" setting.
6. Open the pot and serve warm. Enjoy it with your loved one!

Nutritional Values (Per Serving):

Calories - 172

Fat – 2.5g

Carbohydrates – 10g

Fiber – 2.5g

Protein – 26g

White Wine Haddock

Prep Time: 5-8 min.

Cooking Time: 8 min.

Number of Servings: 2

Ingredients:

- 4 green onions
- 1 cup white wine
- 4 fillets of haddock
- 2 lemons
- Pepper and salt as per taste preference
- 2 tablespoons olive oil
- 1-inch fresh ginger, chopped

Directions:

1. Rub the olive oil into the fish fillets and sprinkle them with pepper and salt.
2. Juice your lemons and zest one lemon.
3. Switch on the pot after placing it on a clean and dry platform.
4. Open the pot lid and place everything except fish in the cooking pot area. Give the ingredients a little stir.
5. Place the fish in a steamer basket and lower it to the liquid. Close the pot by closing the top lid. Also, ensure to seal the valve.
6. Press "Manual" cooking function and set cooking time to 8 minutes. It will start cooking after a few minutes. Let the pot mix cook under pressure until the timer reads zero.
7. Press "Cancel" cooking function and press "Quick release" setting.
8. Open the pot and serve warm with the veggie salad or rice. Enjoy it with your loved one!

Nutritional Values (Per Serving):

Calories - 274

Fat – 8.5g

Carbohydrates – 5.5g

Fiber – 1.5g

Protein – 32g

Tangy Crabs

Prep Time: 5 min.

Cooking Time: 3 min.

Number of Servings: 2

Ingredients:

- 2 tablespoons fish sauce
- ¼ cup butter, melted
- ½ cup water
- 1 tablespoon lemon juice
- ¼ teaspoon salt
- 1-½ pounds. crabs
- ¼ cup minced garlic

Directions:

1. Switch on the pot after placing it on a clean and dry platform.
2. Place crabs in an Instant Pot then season with salt and garlic. Mix the fish sauce and add butter over the crabs then pour water. Give the ingredients a little stir.
3. Close the pot by closing the top lid. Also, ensure to seal the valve.
4. Press "Manual" cooking function and set cooking time to 3 minutes. It will start cooking after a few minutes. Let the pot mix cook under pressure until the timer reads zero.
5. Press "Cancel" cooking function and press "Quick release" setting.
6. Open the pot; top with lemon juice and serve warm. Enjoy it with your loved one!

Nutritional Values (Per Serving):

Calories - 264

Fat – 18g

Carbohydrates – 6.5g

Fiber – 0.5g

Protein – 17g

Mussels Tomatino

Prep Time: 8-10 min.

Cooking Time: 3 min.

Number of Servings: 2

Ingredients:

- ½ cup white wine
- ½ tablespoon dried parsley
- ½ tablespoon pepper
- 2 pounds fresh mussels, cleaned and rinsed
- 1 cup diced tomatoes
- Salt as per taste preference

Directions:

1. Switch on the pot after placing it on a clean and dry platform.
2. Pour the tomatoes into the Instant Pot with the juices and add the wine. Add the pepper, salt, and parsley.
3. Place the mussels in a steamer basket and lower it to the liquid.
4. Close the pot by closing the top lid. Also, ensure to seal the valve.
5. Press "Manual" cooking function and set cooking time to 3 minutes. It will start cooking after a few minutes. Let the pot mix cook under pressure until the timer reads zero.
6. Press "Cancel" cooking function and press "Quick release" setting.
7. Open the pot and serve warm with garlic bread. Enjoy it with your loved one!

Nutritional Values (Per Serving):

Calories - 446

Fat – 10.5g

Carbohydrates – 22.5g

Fiber – 2g

Protein – 55g

Sweet Caramel Salmon

Prep Time: 8-10 min.

Cooking Time: 10 min.

Number of Servings: 2

Ingredients:

- 2 tablespoons brown sugar
- 1-tablespoon fish sauce
- 2 tablespoons soy sauce
- ¾ pound. salmon fillets
- 1-teaspoon vegetable oil
- 1 tablespoon lemon juice
- ¼ teaspoon pepper
- ½ teaspoon ginger
- ¼ teaspoon lemon zest

Directions:

1. Season the salmon with pepper and salt. Set aside. In a bowl mix the vegetable oil with brown sugar, fish sauce, soy sauce, ginger, lemon zest, and lemon juice.
2. Switch on the pot after placing it on a clean and dry platform. Press "Sauté" cooking function.
3. Open the pot lid; add the oil mix in the pot; cook for 2 minutes to caramelize. Add the salmon.
4. Close the pot by closing the top lid. Also, ensure to seal the valve.
5. Press "Manual" cooking function and set cooking time to 5 minutes. It will start cooking after a few minutes. Let the pot mix cook under pressure until the timer reads zero.
6. Press "Cancel" cooking function and press "Natural release (NPR)" setting. It will take 8-10 minutes for natural pressure release.
7. Open the pot and serve warm with the liquid. Enjoy it with your loved one!

Nutritional Values (Per Serving):

Calories - 294

Fat – 12.5g

Carbohydrates – 11g

Fiber – 0.5g

Protein – 34g

Rosemary Salmon

Prep Time: 8-10 min.

Cooking Time: 10 min.

Number of Servings: 2-3

Ingredients:

- 4 Roma tomatoes
- 2 lemons
- ½ cup chopped shallots
- 4 salmon filets
- 2 cups water
- 4 sprigs rosemary
- Pepper and salt as per taste preference

Directions:

1. Slice the tomatoes and the lemons. Make two foil pouches by adding two pieces of salmon over each.
2. Arrange the salmon down on the foil and mix with pepper and salt. Add other remaining ingredients equally.
3. Fold up the foil, so it creates a secure package. Switch on the pot after placing it on a clean and dry platform.
4. Pour the water into the pot. Arrange the trivet inside it; arrange the pockets over the trivet.
5. Close the pot by closing the top lid. Also, ensure to seal the valve.
6. Press "Manual" cooking function and set cooking time to 10 minutes. It will start cooking after a few minutes. Let the pot mix cook under pressure until the timer reads zero.
7. Press "Cancel" cooking function and press "Quick release" setting.
8. Open the pot and serve warm. Enjoy it with your loved one!

Nutritional Values (Per Serving):

Calories – 292

Fat – 22g

Carbohydrates – 13g

Fiber – 2g

Protein – 54.5g

Artichoke Dip with Nachos

Prep Time: 55-60 min.

Cooking Time: 20 min.

Number of Servings: 2

Ingredients:

- 8 medium sized artichokes, make halves
- 2 garlic cloves, minced
- ¾ cup plain yogurt
- ¾ teaspoon salt
- ¼ teaspoon ground pepper
- ½ cup grated ricotta cheese
- ½ lemon
- ½ cup cannellini beans, soaked for about 4 hours
- 1 cup vegetable broth
- Nachos to serve

Directions:

1. Boil artichokes in water for 30 minutes in a pan. Remove the leaves and discard the chokes.
2. Switch on the pot after placing it on a clean and dry platform.
3. Open the pot lid and place the garlic cloves, lemon, vegetable broth, artichokes, and beans in the cooking pot area. Give the ingredients a little stir.
4. Close the pot by closing the top lid. Also, ensure to seal the valve.
5. Press "Manual" cooking function and set cooking time to 20 minutes. It will start cooking after a few minutes. Let the pot mix cook under pressure until the timer reads zero.
6. Press "Cancel" cooking function and press "Natural release (NPR)" setting. It will take 8-10 minutes for natural pressure release.
7. Open the pot. Mix the yogurt, ground pepper, salt, and cheese and mix well.
8. Add these ingredients to a blender and combine until it forms a smooth paste. Serve along with some nachos.

Nutritional Values (Per Serving):

Calories - 188

Fat – 2.5g

Carbohydrates – 29.5g

Fiber – 13g

Protein – 14g

Cheesy Asparagus

Prep Time: 8-10 min.

Cooking Time: 3 min.

Number of Servings: 2

Ingredients:

- ½ pound asparagus spears
- 5-ounces sliced prosciutto

Directions:

1. Wrap the prosciutto slices around the asparagus.
2. Switch on the pot after placing it on a clean and dry platform.
3. Pour 2 cups water into the pot. Arrange the trivet inside it; arrange the asparagus over the trivet.
4. Close the pot by closing the top lid. Also, ensure to seal the valve.
5. Press "Manual" cooking function and set cooking time to 3 minutes. It will start cooking after a few minutes. Let the pot mix cook under pressure until the timer reads zero.
6. Press "Cancel" cooking function and press "Natural release (NPR)" setting. It will take 8-10 minutes for natural pressure release.
7. Open the pot and serve warm. Enjoy it with your loved one!

Nutritional Values (Per Serving):

Calories - 124

Fat – 4g

Carbohydrates – 5.5g

Fiber – 2g

Protein – 17g

Honey Carrots

Prep Time: 10-15 min.

Cooking Time: 5 min.

Number of Servings: 2

Ingredients:

- 1 tablespoon Dijon mustard
- 1 tablespoon honey
- ¼ teaspoon paprika
- 1 teaspoon garlic, minced
- ½ teaspoon ground cumin
- ½ pound carrots
- 1 tablespoon butter
- Pepper and salt as per taste preference
- Dash of hot sauce

Directions:

1. Take the carrots and cut into quarters lengthwise and then cut each quarter in half.
2. Switch on the pot after placing it on a clean and dry platform.
3. Pour 1 cup water into the pot. Arrange the trivet inside it; arrange the carrots over the trivet.
4. Close the pot by closing the top lid. Also, ensure to seal the valve.
5. Press "Manual" cooking function and set cooking time to 2 minutes. It will start cooking after a few minutes. Let the pot mix cook under pressure until the timer reads zero.
6. Press "Cancel" cooking function and press "Quick release" setting.
7. Transfer carrots to a plate.
8. Empty the pot, pat the pot dry. Press "Sauté" cooking function.
9. Open the pot lid; add the butter and other in the pot; cook for 30 seconds.
10. Press "Cancel" and add the carrots. Toss well and serve!

Nutritional Values (Per Serving):

Calories - 138

Fat – 6g

Carbohydrates – 21g

Fiber – 3.5g

Protein – 1.5g

Bean Jalapeno Dip

Prep Time: 8-10 min.

Cooking Time: 30 min.

Number of Servings: 2

Ingredients:

- 1 cup dried pinto beans, rinsed
- ½ teaspoon paprika
- 1 jalapeno, seeded
- 2 cloves garlic, chopped
- ½ teaspoon chili powder
- ½ teaspoon cumin
- 1 medium onion, quartered
- ¼ teaspoon black pepper
- ¼ cup salsa
- ½ teaspoon salt
- 1 ½ cups water

Directions:

1. Switch on the pot after placing it on a clean and dry platform.

2. Open the pot lid and place the above-mentioned ingredients in the cooking pot area. Give the ingredients a little stir.

3. Close the pot by closing the top lid. Also, ensure to seal the valve.

4. Press "Manual" cooking function and set cooking time to 28 minutes. It will start cooking after a few minutes. Let the pot mix cook under pressure until the timer reads zero.

5. Press "Cancel" cooking function and press "Quick release" setting.

6. Open the pot and blend in a blender to make a smooth paste. Enjoy with your favorite crackers or tortilla chips.

Nutritional Values (Per Serving):

Calories - 288

Fat – 2g

Carbohydrates – 26.5g

Fiber – 11g

Protein – 21g

Nutty Chocolate Fudge Balls

Prep Time: 5 min.

Cooking Time: 5 min.

Number of Servings: 2

Ingredients:

- ½ cup walnuts
- ½ cup almonds
- 1 teaspoon vanilla
- 1 12-ounce package chocolate chips, semi-sweet
- 1 14-ounce can of condensed milk
- 2 cups water

Directions:

1. Combine the milk and chocolate chips in a medium bowl. Cover it with aluminum foil.
2. Switch on the pot after placing it on a clean and dry platform.
3. Pour the water into the pot. Arrange the trivet inside it; arrange the bowl over the trivet.
4. Close the pot by closing the top lid. Also, ensure to seal the valve.
5. Press "Manual" cooking function and set cooking time to 5 minutes. It will start cooking after a few minutes. Let the pot mix cook under pressure until the timer reads zero.
6. Press "Cancel" cooking function and press "Quick release" setting.
7. Remove the bowl and mix in the nuts and vanilla. Prepare unformed balls and arrange onto wax paper and allow to cool. Enjoy!

Nutritional Values (Per Serving):

Calories - 156

Fat – 8g

Carbohydrates – 18g

Fiber – 0.5g

Protein – 3.5g

Mouthwatering Raisin Apples

Prep Time: 5 min.

Cooking Time: 10 min.

Number of Servings: 2

Ingredients:

- 3 tablespoons raisins
- ¼ cup sugar
- ¼ cup red wine
- 2 apples, cored
- ½ teaspoon cinnamon

Directions:

1. Switch on the pot after placing it on a clean and dry platform.
2. Open the pot lid and place the above-mentioned ingredients in the cooking pot area. Give the ingredients a little stir.
3. Close the pot by closing the top lid. Also, ensure to seal the valve.
4. Press "Manual" cooking function and set cooking time to 10 minutes. It will start cooking after a few minutes. Let the pot mix cook under pressure until the timer reads zero.
5. Press "Cancel" cooking function and press "Natural release (NPR)" setting. It will take 8-10 minutes for natural pressure release.
6. Open the pot and serve warm. Enjoy it with your loved one!

Nutritional Values (Per Serving):

Calories - 377

Fat – 0g

Carbohydrates – 62g

Fiber – 11.5g

Protein – 3.5g

Chocolate Ramekins

Prep Time: 5-8 min.

Cooking Time: 10 min.

Number of Servings: 2

Ingredients:

- 2 ounces semi-sweet chocolate, chopped
- ½ teaspoon instant coffee
- ½ teaspoon vanilla extract
- 3 tablespoons all-purpose flour
- 1 egg yolk
- 1 egg
- ½ tablespoon sugar
- ¼ cup butter
- ½ cup confectioner's sugar
- ⅛ teaspoon salt

Directions:

1. Grease two ramekins and coat them with the sugar.
2. In a mixing bowl, mix the butter and chocolate. Add the confectioners' sugar and combine well.
3. Whisk in the egg yolk, egg, vanilla, and coffee. Add the salt and flour; combine again. Divide into the ramekins.
4. Switch on the pot after placing it on a clean and dry platform.
5. Pour 2 cups water into the pot. Arrange the trivet inside it; arrange the ramekins over the trivet.
6. Close the pot by closing the top lid. Also, ensure to seal the valve.
7. Press "Manual" cooking function and set cooking time to 9 minutes. It will start cooking after a few minutes. Let the pot mix cook under pressure until the timer reads zero.
8. Press "Cancel" cooking function and press "Quick release" setting.
9. Open the pot; take out the ramekins and top with some powdered sugar. Enjoy it with your loved one!

Nutritional Values (Per Serving):

Calories - 561

Fat – 32.5g

Carbohydrates – 58g

Fiber – 2.5g

Protein – 7g

Wonder Wine Pears

Prep Time: 5 min.

Cooking Time: 10-12 min.

Number of Servings: 2

Ingredients:

- ¼ bottle of your choice of red wine
- 1 piece of ginger
- 1 clove
- 2 pears, peeled
- ½ cup sugar
- 1 cinnamon stick

Directions:

1. Switch on the pot after placing it on a clean and dry platform.
2. Open the pot lid and place the above-mentioned ingredients in the cooking pot area. Give the ingredients a little stir.
3. Close the pot by closing the top lid. Also, ensure to seal the valve.
4. Press "Manual" cooking function and set cooking time to 6 minutes. It will start cooking after a few minutes. Let the pot mix cook under pressure until the timer reads zero.
5. Press "Cancel" cooking function and press "Quick release" setting.
6. Open the pot and carefully take out the pears, setting them aside.
7. Switch the pot to sauté and let the liquid cook until it reduces by half quantity.
8. Drizzle the hot juice over the pears; serve warm!

Nutritional Values (Per Serving):

Calories - 328

Fat – 3g

Carbohydrates – 38.5g

Fiber – 6g

Protein – 2g